Rhythm of the Tides

The Fisheries of Grand Manan

Tim Peters

A TIM PETERS BOOK

Published by Tim Peters Photography
<www.timpeters.com>
BOOKS@timpeters.com

Photographs Copyright © 2000 Tim Peters
Captions, Picture Titles and Text © 2000 Tim Peters
Map Page Design: Copyright © 1997 Dan Leadvaro
Captions and Copy Edited by John Pratt
Production Coordinator, Marstin E. Hastings

First Printing, July 2000

Library of Congress Cataloging-in-Publication Data

Peters, Tim
     RHYTHM OF THE TIDES: THE FISHERIES OF GRAND MANAN
     /Tim Peters
          p. cm.

     ISBN 0-9704008-0-2

     1) Grand Manan—Pictorial Works. 2) Grand Manan, Bay of
     Fundy, New Brunswick (Canada)—Description and Travel
     3) Bay of Fundy, Grand Manan (Canada)—Fisheries

Printed in the United States by
Spectrum Printing and Graphics, Auburn, Maine

Cover: *SETTING TRAPS*, Bay of Fundy, November, 1995
Back: *THE SMOKED HERRING*, Seal Cove, September, 1993

Acknowledgements

I would like to express my sincere gratitude to all Grand Mananers, especially those mentioned below who welcomed me aboard their boats and into their businesses and homes, answered my many queries, and lent a helpful hand. Your hospitality, humility, patience and strength have added something special to my journeys to your island.

—Tim Peters

Vernon Bagley
Kathleen Blanchard, QLF
Stacy Brown
Liz Compton
Deborah Daggett
Douglas Daggett
Wendy Dathan
Celia Fleet
Roland & Flora Flagg
Sandy Flagg
Mervin Fudge
Bonny Gaskill
Dorothy Gaskill
Grand Manan Museum
David Green
Fisher Green
Mark Green
Maurice Green
Winston Green
Brian Guptill
Gary Guptill

John Guptill
Donald Hatt
Glenita Hettrick
Wayne Ingalls
Betty Ingersoll
John L. Ingersoll
Mark Ingersoll
Mathew Ingersoll
Michael Ingersoll
Shirley Ingersoll
Jim Leslie
Sandy Linton
Edward McLean
Myron Morse
Beaver Mullen
Dale Parker
Richard Rice
Troy Russell
Philip Small
Bryan J. Walker
Tom Wetzell

GRAND MANAN ISLAND

PROVINCE  NEW BRUNSWICK

Indian Beach

Ashburton Head

Whale Cove

North Head

Swallow Tail

Pettes Cove

Dark Harbour

Long Island Bay

Long Island

Little Dark Harbour

Castalia

Woodwards Cove

Nantucket Island

Priest Cove

Great Duck Island

Thoroughfare

Andys Ledge

Grand Harbour

Chalk Cove

Ingalls Head

Fish Fluke Point

Long Pond Beach

Seal Cove

Bradford Cove
Hay Point

Harrington
Cove

Wood Island

White Head Island

Southwest Head

Deep
Cove

Three Islands

SOUTHERN HEAD REEF
44° 34' 45" N • 66° 56' 45" W

MURR LEDGES
44° 30' 10" N • 66° 51' 10" W

POPULATION: 2,800
LATITUDE: 44° 42' 30" N • LONGITUDE: 66° 47' 20" W
AREA: 137 SQUARE KILOMETERS • PARAMETER: 76 KILOMETERS

FLOWING TIDE
SEAL COVE SAND BEACH

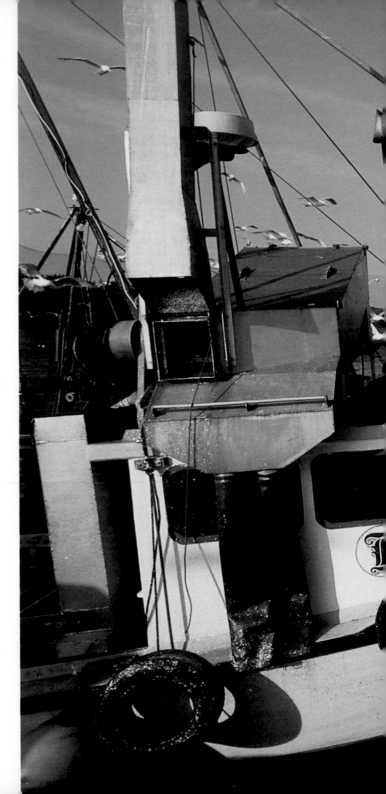

CATCHING A BOW LINE
IRON LADY WEIR

A crewman aboard the herring pumper *Greta & Sons'* is seen catching a bow line from the approaching herring carrier *Strathburn*. Together, their task will be to tie up inside the Iron Lady Weir and pump out the entrapped herring for transport to the Connors Bros. processing plant at Blacks Harbour or Seal Cove. A familiar site around Grand Manan when the herring are running, the act of seining a weir is a static approach to harvesting fish, but effective nonetheless.

ABANDONED LIGHT
FISH FLUKE POINT

WEATHERED HULLS
CHALK COVE

BAGLEY'S POTATO PATCH
SEAL COVE

MUM'S HOUSE

CASTALIA

SEASIDE COTTAGE
CASTALIA

Grand Manan was first settled by United Empire Loyalists in 1784. They migrated from the newly formed United States, seeking a safe haven for their families in Nova Scotia after the American Revolution. Their enacting of English laws and language in the Fundy region quickly led to the formation of New Brunswick within the same year. Farming and fishing were immediately undertaken as a means of sustenance. The island's timbers held the promise of straight keels and spars for shipbuilding.

August Moon
Swallow Tail Light

PORTRAIT OF A LIGHTKEEPER
SEAL COVE

Forsaken Weir Stakes
Long Pond Beach

Down 'n the Creek
Seal Cove

December Storm
Swallow Tail

An easterly gale quickly tosses the waters of the Bay of Fundy and deposits a fresh blanket of snow at Swallow Tail. Sometimes called a "trap smasher" by the island's fishermen, severe storms can pound Grand Manan's eastern shoreline several times a year, fouling boats and gear and temporarily shutting down the island's fishing fleet.

Deadwood
Hay Point

AFTER THE SQUALL
SOUTHWEST HEAD

Rhythm of the Tides

My first earnest journey to Grand Manan Island began in 1995. In the cold and dark of a November morning I arrived at Seal Cove after a sleepless night of tossing and turning. As I trudged down the steel wharf looking for the lobster boat *Mearl Maid,* the smell of diesel fumes was in the air as the purr of marine engines heralded the start of another day at the working waterfront.

Climbing down the wharf ladder, I stepped gently onto the lobster boat's washboard and was met by sternman Beaver Mullen. After a quick introduction, he instructed me to manœuver around the mass of lobster traps overflowing the afterkid and make my way to the wheel house. This I did gingerly, photo equipment in hand. Inside, skipper Fisher Green was warming *Mearl Maid's* engines, turning on the boat's electronics and preparing for the first day of the fall lobster season. We shook hands and made small talk while lines were hauled aboard as the boat pulled away from the wharf.

I made several quick flash pictures as the boat left the shelter of the wharf at Seal Cove under darkness, steering for the ceremonial start line and shotgun blast signaling the start of another lobster season. As we motored onto the bay toward the Murr Ledges, the light began to build. The cloud cover in the western sky was the first sign of an approaching front and rougher seas on the horizon. The weather added a rich texture to the sky which balanced the vastness of the waters on the open bay. The sun hung low and provided an exquisite luminosity found especially in late fall. It was clearly time to photograph.

"You've got sea-legs!" shouted sternman Troy Russell, referring to an ability to keep my balance—cameras in hand—as the lobster boat rode the steady roll on the bay. He also remarked that I was wearing green rubber boots: the ubiquitous footwear that seems to be on the feet of all Grand Manan fishermen. Was this landlubber accepted by crew members? It certainly felt that way!

Experiences aboard *Mearl Maid* gave me a degree of insight into the courage and diligence it takes to fish for a living. It left me yearning for more opportunities to observe and photograph other fishermen at work, and compelled me to complete the cycle of the island's seasonal fisheries.

Over the next four years I would have the privilege to photograph aboard many boats, and freely roam the intertidal zones of Grand Manan Island for interesting pictures and insights.

My first introduction to Grand Manan Island had come via a scuttled sailing trip on the Bay of Fundy in 1993. Our party decided to make the best of the adverse circumstances and visit the island anyway, taking the ferry from Blacks Harbour. We ended up spending three enjoyable days camping at Anchorage Park and exploring the island's raw beauty. While on the prowl for fresh seafood, I noticed a sign on the main road through Woodwards Cove which read, "John L. Ingersoll & Sons' Fresh & Smoked Fish." It was there that I met and befriended islander Mark Ingersoll, a seventh generation Grand Mananer whose ancestor, Jonathon Ingersoll, settled on the island in 1790, after leaving Massachusetts. Since our chance meeting, I have consulted with him on many occasions, and he has been instrumental in my introduction to many of Grand Manan's fishermen.

I was compelled to photograph through many of Grand Manan's fishing seasons, always striving to capture the character and mood of my subjects with a sense of place and rhythm. The photographs began to accumulate and it became evident that a body of work was emerging that needed to be seen in its entirety. After reviewing the imagery with colleagues and editors, the idea for a book began to take shape and the concept for *RHYTHM OF THE TIDES* was born. The name has deep meaning to me; it is representative of the methodical and relentless way in which the islanders live and harvest the resources of the bay. Even those who don't fish must acknowledge the tide's ebb and flow affects everyone on Grand Manan. The Fundy tides have shaped peoples' lives as much as they continue to form the shoreline of the bay. Fortunes have been made by the bounty they can bring. Any serious weir fisherman will attest to that.

The Island is a living example of a fishing community that proudly supports itself through diversification and perseverance. This is truly the inspiration for the photographs!

—TIM PETERS

23

WEIR STAKES AND TWINE
FIRST VENTURE WEIR

SALMON CAGES
DARK HARBOUR

ATLANTIC SALMON
WOODWARDS COVE BREAKWATER

SHOVELING FEED

ANDYS LEDGE

WORKING THE CAGES
ANDYS LEDGE

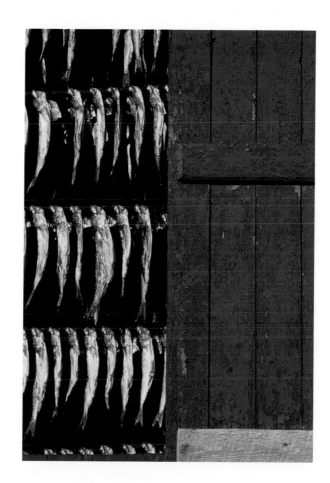

THE SMOKED HERRING
SEAL COVE

The transition to farming Atlantic salmon has provided renewed stability for many Grand Manan fishermen. Feeding fish at a salmon site has replaced the time-honoured, seasonal tradition of smoking herring—once a sure measure of dependability and prosperity for generations of islanders.

PAST AND PRESENT
WOODWARDS COVE

Assembled salmon cages—symbols of the new cash crop fishery—await the uplifting tide at Woodwards Cove. During Grand Manan's heyday of herring (1870-1940), thirty-eight separate smoked herring stands lined the shoreline here, providing plentiful employment as billowing smoke penetrated the entire village. It was during this teeming time that a record 1.85 million boxes of fish were exported in 1891, establishing the island as the foremost supplier of smoked herring. One-hundred and six years later, in the fall of 1997, the very last sticks of herring were hung in the smoke house "bays" at John L. Ingersoll & Sons', and the fish taken down and "boned-out."

TENDING THE SMOKEHOUSE FIRES
WOODWARDS COVE

Ingersoll's Smoke Shed
Woodwards Cove

A light moment warms the air at the John L. Ingersoll and Sons' boning shed in Woodwards Cove. "It's a seasonal job," says Dorothy Gaskill, "and something you have to grow up with. Today's young kids don't like the smell much. They come into the shed hangin' onto their noses!" Boning herring takes quite a bit of manual dexterity that can be rough on the hands. "There's a knack to it, really. You got to know how to wiggle it to get the bone out. 'Cause if you don't, you leave lots of fish." For several generations, Grand Manan women boned herring and were the industry's most dependable source of labour. During the peak years from 1870 to 1940, herring was regularly brought to the homes of many women, especially those with small children and those who were housebound.

THE HERRING BONERS
WOODWARDS COVE

Periwinkle Sacks
Harrington Cove

Periwinkles are accessible to anyone adventurous enough to comb Grand Manan's intertidal zones and pick them. They are best exposed during the twice monthly spring tides, and require only a reliable pair of rubber boots and the willingness to bend down and forage amongst the exposed seabed. The additional income their harvest brings makes them a valuable resource for pickers of all ages on the island.

INTERTIDAL ZONE
PRIEST COVE

THE PERIWINKLE SHED
CASTALIA

DULSE DORIES
DARK HARBOUR POND

Dulse Roll
Castalia

"When the old fellers used to dulse," says Sandy Flagg, "the seawall was thick with wooden cabins the dulsers used as seasonal camps from April to October." Four cable winches are spread out and mounted along the sloping seawall to haul dories from the pond over the 120 meter natural formation to the open waters of Grand Manan Channel. From here they set out in their dories to roam the backside of the island in search of the high quality dulse that grows along the western shore's intertidal zone. Picking dulse can be a hazardous occupation. The large, round and slippery rocks make it difficult to manœuver on the beach and painful falls are commonplace. The water is always in the back of a picker's mind as conditions can often change quickly. Getting stranded on the rocks with a rising tide and a swamped dory can be deadly. "You've got to get your dory off the beach. It's the main concern!" says Flagg.

DAWN CROSSING
DARK HARBOUR POND

Dulse Camps
Dark Harbour Seawall

Launching a Dory
Dark Harbour Seawall

HANDLINE HOOKS
GRAMPS' KIDS

LANDING A POLLOCK
FINNEGANS

HIGH FLYERS
GLIDE ROCKS

WINCHING THE GILLNET

GLIDE ROCKS

POLLOCK AND CODFISH
GLIDE ROCKS

GILLNETTING

GLIDE ROCKS

PURSE SEINERS
BAY OF FUNDY

Purse seiners bob in the calm waters off the eastern shoreline of Long Island as twilight lingers over the Bay of Fundy. Frequently leaving the wharf at sunset, the herring fishermen begin searching for fish at nightfall. The pursuit of herring intensifies as the light-sensitive fish begin to rise from the depths and move into darkening shoal water to feed. Averaging sixty-five feet stem to stern, the purse seiner is large enough to hold and transport seventy-five tons of herring, a design feature that has proven to be a hedge against restrictive government catch quotas and low fish prices.

HERRING CARRIERS
NORTH HEAD WHARF

RAFTED PURSE SEINERS
NORTH HEAD WHARF

In his thirty-seven years on the Bay of Fundy, Maurice Green has experienced quite an evolution in herring fishing. He vividly remembers how cold it was on deck as a young spotter, especially when there was fog. "You leaned off the bow and looked for the glow of the herrin' in the water, and believe me, it was plain as day!" he says, referring to the shimmering phosphorescence of the fish. Green bought his first herring boat in 1967, an open deck fifty-two footer. "In those days it was a wide open fishery. The boats were smaller and very few carried their own herrin'. In 1966, Juddy Guptill's boat, the *Sarah & Stewart,* alone caught 12,000 tons. That's more than the entire nine boat quota last year! Fishin' goes in cycles. In order to make a decent living a Grand Manan fisherman has to be in three or four different fisheries."

At the Wheel of *Fundy Mistress*
Long Island Bay

TIGHTENING GEAR
FUNDY MISTRESS

Pumping Herring
Fundy Mistress

Runnin' Twine
Woodwards Cove

DRYING WEIR TWINE
CASTALIA MARSH

WEIR STAKES
SEAL COVE

THE RESTING WEIR
MURR LEDGES

SEINING THE VICTORY WEIR
LONG ISLAND BAY

The circular pattern of the herring weir is a precise combination of wooden stakes driven into the seabed and sheathed with netting and twine. Strategically placed in shoal water and favoured by the flowing tide, the fish-fence is designed to trap migrating herring as they move along the coastline. Primitive brush weirs were first used by the Migmag and Passamaquoddy peoples in the Bay of Fundy region. European settlers improved the brush weir and introduced the design so typical around Grand Manan Island today.

THE DRY UP
BRADFORD COVE WEIR

PORTRAIT OF A WEIRMAN
WHALE COVE

LOADING HERRING
STRATHBURN

Pumping Herring
Eel Brook Weir

PURSING THE SEINE
IRON LADY WEIR

SPREADING SALT
STRATHBURN

SALTED HERRING
STRATHBURN

HERRING ROE
STRATHBURN

HERRING CARRIER
BAY OF FUNDY

A herring carrier rides low in the water with a load of fish as she passes Pettes Cove, sailing for Blacks Harbour. Her graceful lines, whitewashed hull, deck and wheelhouse are a constant presence and pleasing site in the waters around Grand Manan, as she hauls herring from weirs and purse seiners throughout the lower Bay of Fundy region to processing plants at Blacks Harbour and Seal Cove. The carriers have earned their reputation as efficient and reliable for fish transport.

CANNING HERRING
SEAL COVE

PROTECTIVE WRAP
SEAL COVE

THE VILLAGE
SEAL COVE

G rand Manan's most southerly community is home to a bustling lobster fleet and the island's last remaining fish packing plant. The surviving smokehouses—relics from a bygone era when the heavy scent of smoking herring filled the air here—now house aquaculture supplies and display plaques designating them as Canadian Historic Sites. Walking over Little Creek toward the breakwater, one is hard-pressed to comprehend the massive amount of herring that was salted, strung and smoked on Grand Manan, then shipped to a world starved for a non-perishable protein supply.

LOBSTER CRATE
THE THOROUGHFARE

SHELTERED COVE
GRAND HARBOUR

LOBSTER BUOYS
WOODWARDS COVE

Tagged Traps
Seal Cove

CAULKING A PLANK
INGALLS HEAD

LOBSTER BOAT REPAIR
INGALLS HEAD

The most seasoned of the Grand Manan lobster fishermen, Fisher Green has spent most of his life on the Bay of Fundy. Working 375 lobster traps keeps the seventy-five year old lobsterman and his two-man crew busy throughout the fall lobster season. "We like to haul Mondays, Wednesdays and Fridays if the weather's good and the tides are right." A lobsterman for nearly sixty years, Green recalls when he first fished alongside his uncle Joe. "It was a different day, a different age. Everything then was committed to memory. By the marks on the land, the tides and ripples, they new exactly where to go and where the shoals were. You went out with a compass and a clock, and there was a lot of dead reckonin' to it," says Green. "We was always glad when we found the Southern Head bell buoy. Then we'd run for another twenty-three minutes and we knew we was home."

FIRST LIGHT
BAY OF FUNDY

THE FIRST TRAPS OF THE FALL SEASON

Mearl Maid

FISHERIES TAG
SEAL COVE

SETTING TRAPS
BAY OF FUNDY

RETRIEVING A TRAP
MEARL MAID

THE THIRD MAN
MEARL MAID

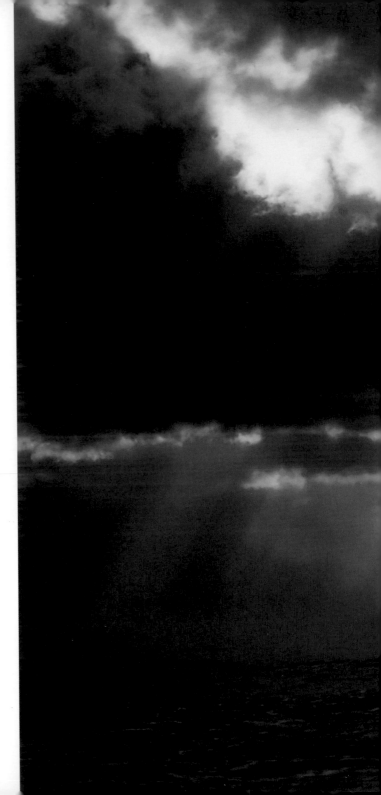

AMIDST THE VAPOUR
MURR LEDGES

A lobster boat hauls traps amidst the vapour on a frigid December morning. Long before daybreak the men rise, layer on their warmest clothing, and head for their boats. Engines turn over and the hum breaks the silence of the still morning air. Soon, the scent of diesel engine exhaust is everywhere as the fishing fleet fans onto the waters of the Bay of Fundy. No one will doubt the hazards of the profession or question the determination it demands from fishermen everywhere.